101
WAYS TO
YOUR
HUSBAND'S
HEART
by
NICK ALLAN

Publishers since 1798

Thomas Nelson Publishers
Nashville • Camden • New York

Illustrated by Ann L. Cummings

Library of Congress Cataloging in Publication Data

Allan, Nick.
  101 ways to your husband's heart.

  No collective t.p. Titles transcribed from individual title pages.
    1. Marriage—Miscellanea.   I. Allan, Rosie. 101 ways to your wife's heart. 1983.   II. Title.   III. Title: 101 ways to your wife's heart.   IV. Title: One hundred one ways to your husband's heart.   V. Title: One hundred and one ways to your husband's heart.   VI. Title: One hundred one ways to your wife's heart.   VII. Title: One hundred and one ways to your wife's heart.

Published in Nashville, Tennessee, by Thomas Nelson, Inc. and distributed in Canada by Lawson Falle, Ltd., Cambridge, Ontario.

Printed in the United States of America.

HQ734.A44   1983   646.7'8   83-13136
ISBN 0-8407-5298-0

    7 8 9 10 11 12 - 97 96 95 94 93 92 91 90 89 88

101
WAYS TO
YOUR
HUSBAND'S
HEART

1

At dinner tonight, reach *under* the table and hold his hand.

2

If you don't care much for sports, really shock him by buying two tickets—one for him and one for you—to a sporting event.

3

Send a jar of peanuts or a package of raisins with him to work for those times when he needs a snack to boost his energy.

4

Some day when you think he needs a little lift or you know he will face mayhem at work, write an endearing note, dab it with perfume, and slip it in his pocket as he leaves.

The week before Father's Day, help the children make a scrapbook that tells and shows what their dad means to them. Use old snapshots, pictures from magazines, original crayon drawings—anything that will show love.

Once or twice a week, watch one of the TV shows he likes with him. Sit next to him—close. Forget about reading, knitting, cracking your knuckles, or chewing gum during the program. Instead, hold his hand and participate in the viewing.

7

Light a candle in the bathroom, fill the tub to the brim, season the water with bath salts, and invite him to share a bath with you. Toast each other with a favorite beverage.

8

During the Christmas season when you feel particularly inspired or nutty, serenade him with carols while he's changing clothes after work.

Visit a travel agency and pick up some brochures on faraway places you know he would like to visit. Snuggle with him in bed, look at the brochures, and dream of those places together.

Don't be hesitant to change your appearance: try a new hairdo, different shades of makeup, a switch in perfume, an unusual nightgown. Keep him guessing and interested.

If exactly what he does at work is a mystery to you, plan to spend a half day with him on the job, just listening and watching. And always encourage him to bring home company newsletters, informative memos, new products he has worked on, and so on.

Next time you go shopping together, stop with him at one of those specialty shops he enjoys—sporting goods, computer/electronics, or video/music. Find out why that stuff intrigues him so much.

13

Buy a kite and, on the first beautiful day of spring, invite him to go with you to a park or grassy field and fly it.

14

If it's been a while since you've shared an evening of fun with other people, invite friends over for cards, other games, or just plain conversation.

15

Buy him a pack of new baseball cards (keep your hands off the bubble gum!) at the grocery store. Give the cards to him some afternoon when he's watching a baseball game on TV.

16

Decide together what is the highest sum of money either of you will spend (without consulting each other) on normal purchases or special items and gifts. The amount might be $5, $25, $100, or $2,500. Abide by the rule at "all costs."

17

Find at least one thing a day—some newspaper story, some idea, some *something*—that is of interest to both of you and talk about it together.

18

Go together to an amusement park or fair. Act like teen-agers. Scream on the roller coaster, play bingo, eat cotton candy. *Insist* that he win you a stuffed animal at the game arcade.

19

Remember when you were dating or first married how you used to sit on his lap and touch his face and hair? Try it again.

20

Next Fourth of July buy him some firecrackers, sparklers, or other fireworks for your own backyard display.

21

Once a month, go to some quiet cafe late at night. Order steaming mugs of coffee. Look into each other's eyes and talk the way you did when you first met.

22

Dig through his old record albums and find one of his oldie-goldie favorites. When he's settled into a chair some evening, play the record for him unannounced. Enjoy reminiscing together about music from the past.

23

When you discuss members of his family, let him do most of the talking. The blood ties are strong, regardless of what he may say to the contrary.

24

Any night of the week, next to the late-night-news slot in his TV program guide, write a note like, "It's time to turn off the TV and turn on your wife. I'm waiting in the bedroom."

25

Do something crazy—like jamming his closet full of
balloons. Next time he opens that door, he should
have a good laugh.

26

Next time he's watching an eagerly awaited sports
event on TV, prepare a very special snack or lunch, sit
down with him, and watch the event while you both
eat.

Buy some chocolate candy bars and hide them in the freezer. The next time he grumbles that there's "nothing sweet in the house," casually say, "Why don't you have one of those candy bars in the freezer?"

Some Saturday morning, ply him with fresh coffee, then drop him off—minus credit cards, checkbook, and piggy banks—at a dealer's where exotic sports cars, vans, motorcycles, or boats are sold. Tell him to browse and that you'll pick him up in an hour.

29

When you go on a trip, secretly bring along one of his favorite books. When time starts to drag and both of you are bored, pull out the book and read to him.

30

Spend at least one weekend alone together each year. No kids, relatives, or friends are allowed—just the original duo. And don't jam the time with activities. Unwind. Sleep. Talk. Eat. Add fuel to your fire.

31

The first brilliant, warm weekend day of spring, dig out the swimsuits and invite him to an afternoon sunbathing session. Talk and doze as you soak up those wonderful rays.

32

Keep an abundant supply of rags on hand. Next time he starts a dirty job on the car or around the house, he'll be thankful for that armful of clean, dry cloths.

33

Six months *after* his last birthday, plan a surprise birthday party for him. It will really be a surprise!

34

Think of new places and times for kisses and hugs—like just *before* dinner, during halftime of a TV football game, in the middle of a fight, while he's digging flower beds, in the checkout line at the grocery store.

35

Call him at work and ask him for a date. Take him to a movie, hold hands, stop for a pizza afterwards. Be sure to top off the evening by "parking"—for old times' sake.

36

Install a small lock on the inside of your bedroom door. Use it at appropriate times. Lock out your cares and the rest of the world.

37

Want some special magic? Curl up next to each other near the wood stove or in front of a blazing fireplace on a cold winter's night. Don't forget the hot chocolate, popcorn, and easy conversation.

38

Surprise him with tickets for the two of you to a concert by one of his favorite entertainers.

39

Buy him a *Superman* comic book and place it on the back of the stool in the bathroom.

40

The night before you celebrate your wedding anniversary, haul out the wedding photographs and reminisce together.

41

Some day when he's shivering, like after shoveling snow or being drenched in a sudden rain shower, help him remove his clothes, wrap him in a bathrobe you've "toasted" in the clothes dryer, and hand him a mug of something hot.

42

If he's been working too hard, call one of his friends and arrange some joint activity they'll both enjoy—like a football game with sideline seats courtesy of you.

43

Return together at least once to the place where he
lived as a boy. Have him give you an exclusive tour of
his favorite boyhood spots and haunts. Encourage him
to share his growing-up experiences with you.

44

Buy him some item that will make him laugh—an
outrageous hat, a loud tie, or a pair of multicolored
boxer shorts.

45

When the kids do or say something cute when he's not around, write it down on a slip of paper and drop it in an unused goldfish bowl. He can pluck one out when he wants a chuckle.

46

Some winter night or rainy afternoon when there's little to do, make a fresh pot of coffee and look at your old family snapshots, slides, or movies together.

47

When a salesman calls asking for "the man of the house," learn what you can about what is being sold and take a phone number—rather than saying, "Why don't you call back when my husband comes home tonight at six?"

48

If he is to be away on a business trip, send a cute card or note ahead to his hotel. A call to him later in the evening might be a nice surprise, too.

In private, practice speaking with a foreign accent (French is very good). When he comes home some night, pretend you are a very young woman, and using your accent, say all kinds of outrageous, obnoxious, and funny things to him, such as: "Ze warre ees over, ma cherie. Let's make loove in ze trenches!" Dressing in an appropriate costume helps.

Remember those times when he really seems eager to share his feelings, to open up? Is there any pattern? Maybe he feels most comfortable really *talking* only around midnight, or at a greasy-spoon restaurant, or alone with you driving at night. Arrange similar circumstances that will encourage him to share his heart.

51

To spice up your life a bit, exchange household duties with each other now and then. If he always mows the grass while you do the grocery shopping on Saturday, switch jobs this week.

52

Bake a chocolate cake to send along with him to work. He can share it with his co-workers. This will make him popular—at least for a day!

Every day try to do at least one thing that will maximize your good qualities, the things about you that drove him wild when you first met. Do you still exercise to stay in shape? How often do you comb your hair and wear makeup when he's around? Do you smile at him as you would a lover? Are you getting enough rest so you have the energy to be a mate?

Take him outside after supper and shoot baskets together.

55

Oldie but goodie: Every now and then, a breakfast in bed—*together*—is a special, appreciated luxury.

56

Buy a book on a topic he enjoys. Read it yourself first, then give it to him and discuss the content after he has read it.

57

Try this for a change of pace—if he has a sense of humor. On a Saturday or perhaps on the second day of your vacation, complain a bit during the day about how lousy you feel—headache, sore back, you know the routine. Retire to bed early, sniffing with an apparent runny nose. Once between the sheets, fake sleep and slip into your birthday suit. When your despondent mate slides under the covers—attack!

58

Hire the boy next door to scrub the garbage cans, give the dog a bath, or do some other menial job your husband hates.

59

Check the classified ads in magazines. Send away for some specialized catalogs for products that would interest him (tools, sporting goods, specialty automobile parts, computer gear, clothing). He'll appreciate a junk mail pile that's not so junky.

60

Call him at the office and tell him you are coming to have lunch with him. When you arrive, throw a tablecloth over his desk, set up a candelabra, and bring out the paper plates, cups, and plastic silverware. His co-workers will think he must be some kind of great husband to deserve such treatment from his wife!

61

After a snowfall and before he has a heart attack, interrupt his shoveling of the driveway and have him help you build a snowman. Have a snowball fight or make angels in the snow. Hot chocolate afterwards, of course.

62

If he is an after-dinner, evening snacker, fix him something very unusual some night—a hot fudge sundae, a taco, oatmeal cookies—a favorite food that will surprise and delight him.

63

On Valentine's Day or some other appropriate occasion, have a plant, flowers, or box of candy delivered to him where he works.

64

If you play an instrument or sing, give him a special, private concert. (If you play or sing badly, he may laugh—but what's wrong with that?)

65

Think of fun, new, endearing names to call him, like "Albatross," "Incredible Hulk," "Burt Reynolds," "Titanic," "Jaws," "Dirty Socks."

66

If you two need some time alone, drive to a state park or similar spot at least forty-five miles from your home. Hike, have a picnic, sit in the sun. You'll have plenty of time to talk.

67

Some evening before he comes home, draw all the drapes, turn the lights on low, and wear some outfit he has always liked—preferably a long gown. When he reaches the door, turn on some of your favorite slow music and dance cheek-to-cheek. Dance the night away.

68

Take a bath and put on perfume at a time of the day when you normally *never* take a bath or put on perfume.

69

If you have children, take some new snapshots of the kids (or dig out a few old ones) and make an original greeting card with those cute, beaming faces. Mail the card to him at work.

70

Once in a while, shore up his ego a bit. Tell him how proud you are of him, of the way he loves you, of how he helps provide for your needs, of the reputation he has at work and in the community. He needs to hear these words from the person who knows him best.

71

On some long winter evening, set up a table and
spread out the pieces of a jigsaw puzzle. Invite him to
help you put it together. Turn off the TV, turn on the
background music!

72

Tie a yellow ribbon on a front yard tree or tack one to
your door, and when he comes home, greet him with a
tickertape welcome and proclaim him "hostage for a
day." After giving your "welcome-home" speech, send
him off to the shower. Next, administer a physical and
mental examination. While dinner cooks, let him catch
up on his old magazines. Encourage him to call a
friend. After he eats, take him off to bed—hostages
are always exhausted.

73

As a very special fun treat, call a local flying service and arrange a half-hour sightseeing plane ride for the two of you. If you are really daring, check out hot air balloon rides.

74

When he arrives home late after working overtime or being away on a business trip, help him take off his coat and shirt. Next, hand him a steaming hot towel; follow this with a cold, icy towel; finish up with a dry towel. Help him slip on one of his very favorite, old, "hang-around-the-house" shirts.

75

Cook him his favorite dish when he least expects it, for example, on the day *after* his birthday.

76

Some evening when you are in an amorous mood and want him to share your outlook, install a colored light bulb in a bedroom lamp. Put on something inviting and inquire if he might want to investigate the new environment.

77

Keep five dollars in change hidden away. When he needs emergency funds for a trip to the store, or he wants to go wash the car, or he desperately wants a newpaper at six o'clock on Sunday morning, you-know-who will end up smelling like you-know-what!

78

Search the TV log to find programs you know will interest both of you. Tell him about these shows and watch them together.

79

Stop by a hardware store with him and insist that he buy one tool he really needs and does not have for jobs around the house.

80

Some rainy afternoon, find a spot in the house where you can hear the rain tapping on the roof or windows. Curl up together and take a nap.

Buy a bag of his favorite candy and place pieces in unusual spots: rolled in his underwear (skip that if his favorite is chocolates!), inside the glove compartment in the car, in his briefcase, in his toolbox, under his pillow.

Call him at work now and then and say nothing; just breathe heavily for thirty seconds! *Cautions:* Be sure it is your husband who answers and, to prevent misunderstandings, always identify yourself before you hang up!

83

At quitting time some Friday afternoon, show up at his place of work unannounced and with a packed suitcase. Abduct him to a room at a nice local motel. Go for a swim, have dinner, talk—you have the idea.

84

Now and then, bring him along when you're shopping for clothes. Ask him what he thinks looks best on you. You might be surprised at his tastes! But is there anyone who should like what you wear more than he does?

85

The next time you're on vacation or at your local swimming pool, goof around a little. Try kissing while under water and other fun things. Have him carry you on his shoulders or pretend you're a shark and take a bite out of him. Let your hearts be young and merry.

86

When you are both feeling silly (and you don't have house guests!), make a "joint appearance" in the shower and perform original and hilarious operatic duets.

87

Look at the annual from his senior year in high school and coax him to elaborate on the things said about him in the "bio" section.

88

Buy a cheap cowboy hat and stick a note in the band inviting him to join you for an afternoon of horseback riding at a local stable.

89

The next time he comes into the house after working outside with his shirt off, let loose with a wild howl and say, "Wow, what a body! Your chest is too sexy for words!"

90

Visit a store stocked with a large assortment of men's colognes and lotions. Sample them and find one he's never tried that you think he will like—and that you like. Slip the bottle onto his shelf in the bathroom.

91

He, like most men, has always yearned for some special toy that he never received as a boy. It might be an electric train, a fire truck with a hose that squirts water, or a BB gun. At Christmas, on his birthday, or on some special occasion, buy the toy for him.

92

Next time the moon is full, go back to the place (or find one like it) where you first gazed at the moon together.

93

Encourage him to invite one of his co-workers home for dinner. You'll learn a lot about what your husband's work life is like.

94

If you have a small child, dress him or her up in the finest clothes and pin on a small sign that reads, "I'm a chip off the old block named (insert husband's name)." Stop by where he works and send the child in to relay some message—like "I love you, Daddy!"

95

On one of those sparkling spring, summer, or fall days, pack a picnic lunch and walk or ride your bicycles to a nearby park or other outdoor spot. Spread a blanket, eat, lie back, and let the breeze float your cares away.

96

Some hot summer afternoon when he's slaving in the yard, bring him a lawn chair, a towel, and a cold glass of lemonade. When he's resting comfortably in the shade, inform him that a baseball game he "really should watch" on TV is about to begin.

97

At least once a week (more often is better), hug him *tight* with both arms, blow in his ear, and say something new (maybe even outrageous) about how much you love him.

98

At least once a year, invite some (if not all) members of his family to your home for a meal or brief visit.

99

Several times a week, do simple physical exercises with him during the commercials of a TV show you're watching.

100

Surprise him by framing one of his achievements—a high-school football letter, an academic award, a picture of his being named "Young _____." Every time he sees it hanging on the wall, he'll think of you.

101

Every now and then, when you think it will do the two of you the most good, interrupt whatever he is doing that he thinks is so doggone important, drag him off to the bedroom, lock the door, and attack!

101

She appreciates the nice special things you do for her, but at least once a day, say those three most wonderful words—"I love you."

99

If your work requires that you travel, surprise her once by secretly making all the arrangements for her to take a trip with you.

100

At some time when she'd least expect it (like January?), you and the kids plan a special surprise Mother's Day. Take her out to breakfast or buy her a corsage or clean up after all the meals or go for a drive.

97

Some morning after you arrive at work, call her and say, "Have a great day! And, by the way, I'll bring supper home tonight!"

98

If you really want to pile up some "points," shine all of her shoes some afternoon while you're watching a game on TV.

95

Sincere compliments are great for her outlook. Tell her—"You look great," or "You're a terrific mother!" or "You do wonders for that nightie!"

96

Make a point of being on hand to unload and carry in the bags when she returns from a major trip to the grocery.

93

Now and then, buy her a box of her favorite candy. The gesture "says" love.

94

Check often to be sure there is plenty of gas in the car she drives.

91

On a beautiful, warm, spring Sunday, plan a picnic at a nearby park. Pick up necessary food items at the nearest deli. Take your Frisbee and blanket.

92

Plan a different family fun evening. For example, make a cassette tape letter to a relative or friend, or record a homemade concert or skit on tape or film for the family archives.

89

On a wedding anniversary, bring out the wedding photos and reminisce. Encourage her to unpack her wedding gown and try it on.

90

If you have young children, mark on the calendar a half day once a month for her to leave the house and do whatever she wants.

87

A change of pace: On her birthday, have a huge bouquet of flowers delivered instead of buying her a present.

88

When you see an advertisement for a nearby crafts or antique show, send it to your wife with an invitation attached asking her to attend the event with you.

85

Buy a long-stemmed red rose on your way home one day. Instead of dragging in the back, ring the bell at the front door. When she opens it, say something like, "Good evening, my sexy sweetheart!" Kiss her passionately.

86

Send her a letter proposing a "snuggle date" for a particular evening. Go to bed early. Snuggle, talk, hold each other.

83

If she's not feeling well, warm up the bed with a heating pad or electric blanket, then send her to bed at least an hour before her normal bedtime.

84

Write a list of all the things you love about her. Seal the list in an envelope and leave it on her pillow.

Once or twice a year, take some photographs of her, the kids, the pets, and you involved in normal activities. Send them to her parents.

Offer to share your hobby with her. You may be shocked by her sudden enthusiasm for photography, collecting baseball cards, or tending tropical fish.

79

Take her to some event she remembers fondly from her childhood—the circus, a fashion show at a department store, a doll house exhibit at a local museum, a county fair. Reminisce together about her girlhood.

80

At an unusual time, like when she's balancing the checkbook, sit down next to her—real close—and say, "Where do you really want to go on our next vacation?" or "Do you think our dog is smart enough to get into obedience school?"

77

Some year on the date you asked her to marry you, recreate that special moment and do again what you did back then. Fun, romantic, and memorable.

78

Buy her the latest book by one of her favorite authors. After dinner hand it to her and tell her to curl up in a chair and read while you clean up.

Drop by a department store and buy her a new perfume—one *you* like.

Pick a night and plan to cook a meal together. Select some new recipes, make out the grocery list, and arrange the table setting together. Both of you should wear aprons while cooking.

73

Have a bottle of bubble-blowing liquid handy at all times for "special moments." Shower her with bubbles when she's talking to a friend on the telephone, polishing her nails, assembling the meatloaf!

74

Stop at a specialty T-shirt shop and have a shirt made with a message just for her. Something like WORLD'S HOTTEST WOMAN, or YOU'RE LOOKING AT AN ANGEL, or I BELONG TO A REAL MAN, or THIS BODY MELTS AT THE SIGHT OF (insert your name).

71

On her birthday, plan a treasure hunt that will lead her to her hidden gift. Make the hunt long and full of laughs!

72

Sneakily, at an unusual time of the year, hang a small leaf of mistletoe on the bedroom ceiling directly above her pillow. When she hops in bed, begin kissing her with unusual passion and persistence. Try to keep a straight face until she catches on to the fun.

69

At Christmastime, go on a shopping trip together. Stop later for a mug of something hot, watch the crowds, listen to the music, talk.

70

If your children are grown and no longer at home, without Mom's knowing, have them come home for a weekend visit, set up a special family "night on the town," or plan a joint vacation.

67

If someone must make a trip to the store for milk or medicine or other essentials at night, tell her to stay safe at home and go out yourself.

68

Make her laugh—dress for bed wearing only a paper sack over your head, leave funny notes in her lingerie, dump bubble bath in the toilet tank.

65

Rent a tuxedo, then make arrangements with a friend to be your chauffeur for an evening. Tell your wife to dress for an elegant night out. Have the chauffeur (dressed in dark suit and cap) pick you two up (even if it's your car). While the "driver" wheels you about town, sit close to each other in the backseat, smile, and relax.

66

Call—or have someone call for you—when you are going to be late for dinner, or at any time when she is expecting you.

63

Plan one project per year that you do together for your children. For example, build a doll house, set up a model train layout, or redecorate a bedroom.

64

Pin a note on her mirror that reads something like "Hello, Beautiful! You're looking at the woman (insert your name) loves with all his heart."

61

For lunch take her to the best delicatessen in town and share a wild and different sandwich.

62

If she has cabin fever due to a sick child or for some other reason, ask her to call a friend and go for a visit, while you take care of things at home.

59

As you ride home from work, try to think of at least one thing that happened during the day to share with her. It might be a joke you heard, a great report on company profits, an interesting conversation with a co-worker.

60

If she enjoys gardening, help her prepare and plant a special bed of her favorite annuals in the spring.

57

Make your wedding anniversary gifts to her unique and memorable—those lists of things you are "supposed" to give (something wood, something paper, something silver) may help you think of original ideas.

58

Buy some bubble bath, and in the evening prepare a hot bath, put a colored bulb in the lamp or lighting fixture, supply soft music with a portable radio, and leave her to soak in luxurious solitude.

55

Once a year, select *together* at least one new spare-time activity you can enjoy as a couple—beach combing, square dancing, bird watching—the list is endless.

56

On some occasion when you must go out of town overnight, call a friend of hers and arrange for the two of them to go out for dinner, see a movie, or just spend an evening talking or working on hobbies.

53

Don your hunting cap or a pith helmet and grab a broom. Inform her that you are going "big cobweb" hunting and remove the cobwebs from the ceilings and corners of every room in the house!

54

Help her shampoo her hair, all the while gently massaging her scalp.

51

Buy a scrapbook or photo album and set aside the first rainy Sunday afternoon to help her fill it with family snapshots and other memorabilia.

52

When the inside of the car she drives becomes littered and the outside resembles a relic from the dust bowl, take charge and clean it up!

49

Christmas night, after the kids are tucked in and you're alone, bring out a specially wrapped package—something small but intimate, just for her from you.

50

Keep her wondering what you might do next—like after she's just rolled her hair and probably isn't feeling too desirable, sweep her off her feet, and carry her to the bedroom, and . . .

47

On one of your quick stops to pick up a few groceries, bring her something she likes that wasn't on the list— a special surprise like a pineapple, the latest "blockbuster" novel, or a gigantic chocolate bar.

48

Together, plan a "far off in the future" project or trip. For example, on your fifth wedding anniversary, start dreaming and planning for a trip to Hawaii on your twenty-fifth!

Buy her a music box that plays a romantic tune that was popular when you two were dating or just married.

If you must be gone overnight frequently, do some things around the house that will make her feel more secure, such as installing dead bolt locks, getting a dog, and installing a phone near her bed.

43

Remember how Nelson Eddy used to serenade Jeanette MacDonald? For a laugh, some morning when you are both waking up, croon a love song to her while you are both still in bed.

44

If you know she's had a really hard day, have her lie down and give her a soothing massage.

Have her dig out the old high-school or college photos and reminisce. Top it off by encouraging her to call an old friend.

On at least one sparkling fall afternoon, switch off the TV football game and go walk with her hand-in-hand through the fallen leaves.

39

Are some of her clothes frayed or looking a bit out of style? Insist that she go shop for a new skirt or blouse.

40

Once a month (at least!) rescue her from the kitchen. Take her and the kids out for a meal on the weekend.

37

Every day, catch her for a good bear hug that lasts at least five seconds. Ten seconds is better. Fifteen seconds is better yet—you have the idea!

38

The next time you're really "burned up" about your boss or excited "out of your socks" about a big project, share these feelings and ideas with her. She longs to know the you *inside* you.

35

Really "freak her out" sometime by picking up your scattered clothing—then picking up hers as well. (Look up the treatment for shock in a first-aid book before trying this one!)

36

Buy a small piggy bank (one that opens easily) and place some extra change in it. Place the bank in the car she drives so she'll have a backup supply of cash for parking, tolls, and telephone calls.

Some Sunday afternoon, take the kids to the park and allow her two or three quiet hours alone in her kingdom.

Stop at a newsstand during the day and pick up a home decorating, hobby, or women's magazine she'd like. Hide it in the sleeve or pocket of her bathrobe.

31

Buy a sack of balloons, inflate them, and write endearing messages on them with a felt tip pen. Then, some day when she's gone, hang, stuff, and hide the balloons all over the house.

32

When you are together in public, walk hand in hand, give her a kiss, wrap your arm around her shoulders.

29

Á la Sherlock Holmes, carefully examine her wedding ring. Repeat the story of how you selected it.

30

If she is sick in bed, make a huge, colorful get-well card (have the kids help) and hang it where she can see it.

Secretly buy a set of satin sheets and pillow cases. Just as secretly put them on your bed. Enjoy her response when she climbs in next to you that night.

Take an hour on your next day off to do some of the little jobs she wants done, such as oiling a squeaky door or hanging a picture.

25

In springtime take her for a walk in the woods. Pick her a bouquet of wild flowers.

26

Tear the movie ads out of the newspaper and attach a note asking her to pick out a movie the two of you can go to. Leave the ad and note on the kitchen table.

23

Walk, jog, bicycle, shoot baskets, swim, play golf or tennis—do something to keep your body healthy and trim. A woman like her deserves a man who looks great!

24

Slip some suggestive, funny, outrageous notes to her into the toilet tissue roll in the bathroom.

If she's frustrated about her weight or physical condition, surprise her with a spa or health club membership, buy her a new aerobic exercise record, or help her set up a diet-exercise routine.

Far in advance (anticipation is half the fun) purchase tickets to a play or concert. Then make *all* the plans for a special evening out. Tell her about it with these wonderful words: "Honey, it's all arranged. All you have to do is be ready!"

19

Buy a very sexy nightgown. Wrap it in a small package and hide it in a breakfast cereal box, or some other place where she'd not expect to find such an item.

20

If she's had a rough week and the laundry pile looks like Mount Everest, tell her you'll "tackle the mountain" and load the washer while she does something else.

If the weather is gloomy and the rains won't go away, rig up an indoor sun lamp, drag out the lawn chairs, and invite her to a bit of indoor sunbathing. Be sure to have tanning lotion, cold drinks, and towels on hand. Cool off with a "swim" in the bathtub. Barbecue hot dogs in the oven.

On at least some of your business trips, plan ahead so that a letter, card, or note will be waiting in the mailbox every day you're away.

Write a newsy letter to her parents or some special friend.

Send her flowers to celebrate a "non-occasion" occasion such as taking the snow tires off the car, the neighbors' finally cutting their lawn, the great lasagna she made last weekend, or sending in the income tax.

13

For Christmas buy a calendar for the next year and circle one date in each month. Include a note that says: "Please plan to spend several hours alone with me on each of the dates circled." Wrap up the calendar and place it under the tree.

14

Now and then sweep her off her feet and carry her across the threshold of your home.

11

If she normally has to get up early every morning (like to take care of the children), give her a great treat by placing a note sealed in an envelope on her pillow. The note should read, "You are invited to sleep in as long as you wish tomorrow morning. This gift compliments of your handsome husband!"

12

Shock her with this one! Some morning at the breakfast table say, "Honey, I don't want to read this boring newspaper this morning. Let's talk instead."

On a cold, rainy, or snowy night—get a blanket, some favorite magazines or a book, and snuggle up together on the couch for a quiet evening of reading.

Call her during the day and read her a verse or two from a favorite romantic poem, such as Elizabeth Barrett Browning's "How do I love thee? Let me count the ways . . ."

On any anniversary of your first date, send her a card with a few "Do you remember how I spilled gravy on your dress?" type notes!

Urge her to invite two or three friends over for a Saturday brunch. You dress up as a waiter and serve the meal. You might even be a singing waiter!

5

Make up some coupons that are good for your help with three unpleasant household chores. Attach them to the broom or inside the door of the cleaning supplies cabinet.

6

On some occasion when she'd least expect it, buy a cake and have it decorated with a message that's cute, funny, or sentimental. The whole family will love the sweet surprise.

Buy one of those large fake noses and secretly slip it on when you two are in bed and the lights are out. Nuzzle her a little. A laugh now and then does everybody some good!

Ask her for a new photograph that you can display on your desk or in your billfold.

Surprise her with some "his and hers" items—
sweaters, T-shirts, jewelry. Let the world know you two
belong together!

Check the yellow pages for an unusual shop she may
have missed—but one you know she'd like. Take her
there and browse together.

101
WAYS TO
YOUR
WIFE'S
HEART

Illustrated by Ann L. Cummings

Copyright © 1983 by Rosie Allan and Nick Allan

Library of Congress Cataloging in Publication Data

Allan, Nick.
  101 ways to your husband's heart.

  No collective t.p. Titles transcribed from individual title pages.
    1. Marriage—Miscellanea. I. Allan, Rosie. 101 ways to your wife's heart. 1983. II. Title. III. Title: 101 ways to your wife's heart. IV. Title: One hundred one ways to your husband's heart. V. Title: One hundred and one ways to your husband's heart. VI. Title: One hundred one ways to your wife's heart. VII. Title: One hundred and one ways to your wife's heart.

Published in Nashville, Tennessee, by Thomas Nelson, Inc. and distributed in Canada by Lawson Falle, Ltd., Cambridge, Ontario.

Printed in the United States of America.

HQ734.A44 1983   646.7'8   83-13136
ISBN 0-8407-5298-0

      7 8 9 10 11 12 - 97 96 95 94 93 92 91 90 89 88

101
WAYS TO
YOUR
WIFE'S
HEART
by
ROSIE ALLAN

Thomas Nelson Publishers
Nashville • Camden • New York